The Secret

Written and Illustrated

by Shelley Davidow

ISBN: 978-1-931061-43-8

Jalmar Press

PO Box 370

Fawnskin, CA 92333

800 429-1192

F: (909) 866-2961

www.jalmarpress.com

For Timothy Caelan Williams, who makes me laugh.

And for Dhyana and her class 5, 2008 at the Shearwater Steiner School, NSW Australia, with love.

Acknowledgements:

My thanks to Cindy Walker at Whole Spirit Press in Colorado for her outstanding vision and ongoing support, and to Mali Kate Biggin-Johnston in Australia, for being such a great reader of the first draft.

About the Author and Illustrator: Shelley Davidow was born in South Africa. Her books for children, young adults and adults have been published in Africa, the UK, the USA and Australia. In 2002 she was nominated by Macmillan/Picador/BBC World for the Macmillan Writer's Prize for Africa, for her young adult book <u>In the Shadow of Inyangani</u>. (Macmillan 2003). She has an MSEd from Sunbridge College in New York and has taught in schools, colleges and universities across the world. She now lives on the East Coast of Australia with her husband and son. Visit www.shelleydavidow.com.

About the Phonetic Readers: The first set of six readers, published in 2006, use simple words that the early reader will easily grasp. The words have been carefully chosen by a reading specialist to help students advance from the short vowels, to the silent "e", to the vowel combinations. <u>The Secret Pet</u>, is the first chapter book in this series. It's a continuation of the phonetically-based principles that focus on the phonetic vowel teams such as ea, ie, oe, ue, digraphs, open and closed syllables and more. <u>The Secret Door</u>, is the second chapter book in this series. It continues with the phonetically-based principles that focus on, ar, or, er, ir, ur, oo, ou, ow, oi, oy, au, aw, and ea words.

About our Reading Specialist: Mary Spotts has been a remedial reading teacher for over fifteen years, taking countless classes and seminars to keep current in the field she loves. Her deep understanding that struggling readers still need good stories—even if the books are phonetically based —has been the inspiration in the creation of these books. Mary has been a constant guide, ensuring that the books address specific phonetic principles while retaining a gently humorous story line.

Table of Contents/ Phonetic Concepts

Chapter 1: A Snarl in the Dark

Nine-year-old Mina could not fall asleep. Her sister, Jo, was already out like a light. It was nine at night, and Mina had read to the end of her book. It was a good book, full of magic. Outside, the summer sky was almost dark, but a full moon lit up her room.

She could see the back yard in the white light of the moon. Then she heard something—a far off sound like a snarl, or a howl.

Mina sat up, and her book fell off the bed. Then she gave a start. "It sounds like there's a dog in the yard. That must be Tim's dog, Ned!" she said. Tim was eleven. He lived next door. Tim had lots of pets. He even had a pet snake, Jake. Sometimes Jake the Snake hid in Tim's shirt and went to school with them all. Mina, Jo and Tim all went to the same school. Jo and Mina loved Tim's pets.

Sometimes Ned, who was a sweet dog, came to play in Mina's yard. "Why would Ned be here at night?" Mina said to Jo.

But Jo was still asleep in the bed next to hers, snoring her eight-year-old head off.

The next moment Mina heard a loud bark. The sound seemed to come from the old workshop, at the back of the house. "Maybe Ned got shut up in the workshop," she said to herself.

Mina got out of bed. She went softly across the carpet and out of her room. Now that she was nine, she wasn't afraid of the dark. She went out of the house into the back yard. Then she heard it again—a loud bark not too far away.

Mina walked across the yard. Her feet were wet, and the moon was big and bright. Its light fell on the old workshop at the back of the house. Mina heard a faint snarl. The sound came from inside the old workshop.

"You should not be creeping across the yard in the dark. It's not smart!"

Mina gave a start and saw the shadow of her little sister.

"It's not dark. And you should be in bed, Jo!"

"Speak for yourself," said Jo and took Mina's arm. "I heard it too."

"I think Ned got shut up in the workshop," said Mina.

"Let's get him out," said Jo.

The two sisters crept around the garden to the workshop. They could hear their parents talking in the living room. The girls peeked into the workshop. All they saw was the big white moon in the dark window. Then they heard it again…a bark and a snarl coming from somewhere inside the workshop.

"Let's get Ned out," said Jo.
The girls went to the door and opened it. The moon cast stark shadows on the ground.

"Come on out, Ned!" Jo said. Ned was not inside. There was a bark again. This time it came from the cellar under the workshop.

Mina took a step forward and stood on something made of wood. She bent down to touch it. Moonlight fell on the wood.

"It's the door to the cellar," Mina said. She had been down there once. It was a tiny room at the bottom of some damp steps. It was used to keep a big, old chest full of Uncle Toby's notes and old books. Uncle Toby was a writer. He lived far across the sea now. When Mina and Jo were very small, Uncle Toby lived close by. He used to tell them bedtime stories that were so good that Mina and Jo wished they were true.

There was a small gap by the trap door where Mina could slip her fingers under the wood. Mina lifted the door. The first few steps were lit up, but the bottom steps were dark. The moon in the sky made it almost as bright as day.

"How did he get in there?" Mina said.

She held the door up and looked in. The smell of earth filled her nose. Then they heard a snarl.

"I'm not going down," said Jo, taking a step backward.

Mina wasn't afraid of a bark in the dark. She knew it was Ned. She took one step into the cellar, then another. "Ned!" she said. "Come on Ned!"

She saw Uncle Toby's trunk of old books and notebooks that were lit up by the moon and stars.

A cold wind blew down the steps. Suddenly Mina felt a warm, furry body brush up against her leg. "Ned! What are you doing down here?"

She felt for his collar. It wasn't there. The furry body gave a short, sharp bark.

"I'm not Ned," he said. "I'm Cal, the red fox."

"Pardon?" Mina said. She bent forward. At first she could hardly see him. Then she saw his bright eyes and pointy nose, and she let out a cry.

"I won't harm you, silly," said Cal.

"What are you doing here?" said Mina.

"Waiting for you," said Cal.

"Oh, dear," said Mina. "Why?"

"I need your help. Do you love a good story?"

"I do! Yes!" said Mina.

"Good! I've got one for you," said Cal. "I've been waiting for at least 30 full moons. Now, tell me, are you good at telling stories?"

"I'm sort of okay," said Mina. "I read a lot. I write a little. I tell Jo stories at night. My Uncle Toby is a really good storyteller. But he's not here."

"Right," said Cal, and his tail flicked from left to right.

"I've never met a speaking fox before," said Mina. "What do you want? How did you get here?"

"I need your help, Mina. I need someone who loves stories. I need help with my story. Come with me. I'm in grave danger. Follow me, and I'll tell you everything."

Mina looked back toward the steps, but she did not see steps behind her. She was on a hill, and moonlight fell on rocks and bushes. A cool wind blew. "Where are we?" she said.

"Not too far from home," said Cal. "You are in a story that your dear Uncle Toby wrote but never finished. You are in the Land of Unfinished Stories. It has been hard to be Cal, the red fox, in a story that has stopped mid-way. I cannot make up the end to my own story. You have to help me!"

"Mina!" shouted Jo from above. "Are you still down in that cellar? Have you found Ned? Come out!"

"I have to go, Cal. I'll be back," said Mina. "I'll come and help you...soon." She turned toward the hill. Then she ran past the rocks, onward, upward and homeward. The next moment the cellar steps were under her feet.

Chapter 2: Cal's Error

The girls ran out of the workshop and across the damp grass.

"What was it?" said Jo. "Tell me, what did you find down there?"

"Come. Let's go back to bed and I'll tell you what I saw." The girls went into their room and got into bed.

"I went through a secret door that wasn't even there," Mina said with big eyes.

"What do you mean?" said Jo.

"Past the cellar wall there was another land. In that land, I found Cal the red fox. He's in one of Uncle Toby's stories!"

"No way," said Jo. "You must be making that up. It's one of your bedtime stories."

"If you like," said Mina, "but this time, it's true."

***

In the morning Mina got out of bed and shook her sister awake.

"Come on, Jo, we have to find the story! It's got to be in the trunk with Uncle Toby's old books."

"I'm tired. I've had the worst night in the world. Your tales of speaking foxes, and secret doors and unfinished stories have worn me out."

"Well, did we find Ned the dog, or not?"

"No," Jo said.

"You have to trust me, Jo. Cal the fox is in torment because Uncle Toby left his story unfinished. I'm going to get Tim to help if you won't come. He's eleven. We need all the help we can get."

"Good luck," Jo said. She pulled the blanket over her head.

Later that day, Tim and Mina were in the workshop. Mina said, "The inventor of the story is my Uncle Toby. His notebooks are kept in the big chest in the cellar. We have to go down there and find Cal's story."

Tim held the trap door open and Mina went down. There stood the chest. She used scissors to cut through thick tape that held the chest shut. Then Mina had to sort out the books.

"Got it!" she said. "Look at this!" Mina ran up the steps with an old notebook in her hands.

They both looked. On the cover of the old notebook Mina read:

"Cal the Red Fox—by T. Williams. That's my uncle," she said.

"This is it!" said Mina.

The children read the notebook, and quickly got lost in the story. Mina read out loud:

> Big Baboon lay in the forest after the fight with his friend, Prince Panther. It was all because of Cal, the red fox. He had made Prince Panther think that his friend Big Baboon wanted the crown. Now all was lost. Cal saw what he had done. He ran far across the plain...

Tim and Mina didn't hear Jo come down the steps. They both jumped with fright.

"Hey!" Mina cried out. "You scared us, Jo!"

"What are you doing?" she asked.

"Look," Tim said. "There's no more. It ends right here where the moon is full:

Cal sat on the plain, forlorn after the storm. The prince would hunt him, and he would forever be his mortal enemy, for Big Baboon was so badly hurt that he was, most likely, dead by now...

"That's so sad. We'll have to come back here tonight after dark," said Mina.

"I want to go with you," said Jo. "I want to know the story."

"You have to trust me then," said Mina.

"Okay, okay! But how can there be a land beyond the cellar door?"

The three children looked at the trap door. "I want to go and see what's down there," said Tim. He went to lift the door. In the daylight, they could see every crack in the steps. "Let me inspect. I'll put the book back," he said in a grown-up way.

"Okay, Inspector," said Mina. "If you find yourself on the top of a hill, come right back here again. But there's nothing there today. I've just been there."

"Okay," said Tim and went down the steps.

"What do you see?" Jo called out.

"A trunk," Tim said, "with books in it. I just put the story of Cal back."

"Is there a secret door that you can't see?" said Jo.

"No," said Tim.

"Is there a hill?" Mina said.

"No, just a blank cellar wall," said Tim.

In no time he was up the steps and out of the cellar.

Mina felt a bit sad. What if it wasn't true? But she knew it was! She also knew that magic could never happen in the bright light of day.

"I think this only happens at night," Mina said. "Let's meet here at nine o' clock, just after dark."

"Last night the moon was full," Jo said. "I think that means something."

"It will still be bright tonight. We will be just fine," said Mina.

"See you at nine," said Tim.

When they met, Mina's worry grew worse. The moon was no longer full, but it was still bright and they could see down into the cellar. Mina went down first, calling out, "Cal, Cal, where are you?"

At the bottom of the steps she found the trunk and a cool, blank wall. She felt the wall, but it was as hard and solid as rock. There was no secret door to a secret land.

Mina came back up the steps and took a look at Jo's face.

"Don't say a word," she said. "I did meet Cal, and it

was real. I don't know why it won't work now."

"Last night the moon was full," said Jo again.

"That's it!" Mina cried. "It has to be a full moon! In the story the moon is full, and it's after a storm."

"I already said that!" said Jo. "It's my idea. The moon has to be full."

"Right!" said Tim. "We have to come back next month. Maybe it will work then. I'd better get home. See you later."

Tim ran home. The girls could hear Ned barking happily in Tim's front yard as he said, "shhhh!" to his dog.

The girls were back in bed before ten.

"Tell me Cal's story," said Jo.

Mina sat up in bed.

"So the prince of the land is a panther, and Prince Panther's best friend is Big Baboon. Anyway, Cal made the prince think that Big Baboon wanted the crown, even though there's an evil rat called the Firman, who really does want the crown. But there's not much about him in the story. So Prince Panther and Big Baboon have this big fight. Big Baboon is almost dead, and Cal runs away when he sees what he's done."

"How can there be a Prince Panther and a Big Baboon in our cellar, Mina?"

"I don't know how that works," Mina said. "How can there be a fox named Cal under our cellar?"

"Maybe there isn't one," said Jo. "Maybe it's just a story."

"It is just a story and it's not finished! That's the point! Somehow I got into the story, and now I want to help!"

"But if Cal did something bad, why should we help him?"

"Because he can't save himself or his friends. And he's sorry for what he did."

Jo's eyes were big in the moonlight. "Uncle Toby made the whole thing Cal's error, but Cal got stuck in the story, and so did everyone else. Cal needs us to help him with his story, or he'll be stuck forever."

"We have to help him then," Jo said, sliding into bed.

"Exactly," said Mina. "Now I can't sleep."

"Force yourself," Jo said, and she began to snore.

Maybe Cal had made the error, Mina thought, but Uncle Toby was Cal's creator. Uncle Toby had made Cal do what he did. If she could go through the secret door and find her way to Cal again, everything could change. Mina did not know how things could change exactly, but she knew they could. She would find out all about Uncle Toby. She did not know where he was and why he had left so many unfinished stories in the trunk. She needed Tim and Jo. Together they could be the creators of the rest of the story. Cal had said so himself.

Chapter 3: The Magic Herb

The moon was perfect and full. A month had gone by. Light fell on the cellar door. It was five minutes past nine.

"Open the trapdoor, Mina," Jo said. Tim stood back as she did so.

"Okay. One person at a time," Mina said, and began to go down the steps. The moon was behind her, and its light made her shadow blacker and longer than the last time.

"Maybe Uncle Toby is dead," Jo said.

"Mom said he's not," said Mina. "He just lives by himself. She said he left the country and never writes anymore. Not even letters. He gave up writing when he could not finish his stories."

"Why?" said Jo.

"Mom said that he wanted to write books for children, but no one wanted to publish his stories, so he gave up. Now he won't write anything. He most likely doesn't want to hear from anyone, even us." Mina said.

"Shhh!" said Tim. "Do you feel that?"

"What?" said the girls together. Was the cellar ahead of them getting lighter?

"The wind," said Tim. "It's blowing harder."

A second later, they heard a bang. The cellar door had shut and the children were suddenly walking down a rocky hill.

"It's true!" said Jo with wonder. "We're on the other side of the secret door!"

"It's the land of the Panther Prince," said Mina, "and Cal."

There was a wide, flat plain in front of them. To the east, there was a glimmer of light in the sky.

"Looks like it's getting lighter," Tim said.

"Where is Cal?" Mina said.

Just then, Tim, Mina and Jo heard a whimper and saw a tuft of amber fur behind a rock. Then the children saw the nose and the ears of a small, red fox.

"You must be Cal," said Jo with big, wide eyes.

"So I am," said the fox. "Mina, who are these people?"

"This is my sister, Jo…"

"And I'm Tim. I live next door."

"Nice to meet you, Jo and Tim. Now, I must confer with Mina by myself. Follow me a little way." Mina did. Then Cal said: "Are Jo and Tim to be trusted?"

"Yes, oh yes," said Mina.

"And do they know my story?" said Cal.

"Some of it, yes."

"We can't linger. Time is short. Tell them to follow us."

The children went after Cal as fast as they could. It was hard to keep up with a running fox. The sky was dim but getting brighter. Trees bent in the wind as they came to a forest.

"Faster," said Cal. "The story ends here."

Near a tree, lay a big, dark shape on the ground. It lay very still.

"What's that?" said Jo.

"This is Big Baboon," said Cal.

"Is he dead?" said Tim.

Just then Big Baboon began to mutter.

"No, he's not," said Cal. "But he will die soon. He's badly hurt from a battle with Prince Panther. All because of my tricks."

Big Baboon began to mutter again.

"Tell me more of your story, Cal," said Jo. Sunlight began to seep through the trees.

Cal was very sad. His ears came forward and made his face pointy. "I told Prince Panther that his best friend, Big Baboon, was after the crown. I told Big Baboon that Prince Panther wanted to fight with him. Big Baboon thought Prince Panther had gone mad, and Prince Panther no longer trusted his friend. So they had a big fight. I did it."

"Why?" asked Jo.

"Because foxes are always seen as vermin in stories," Cal said. "Foxes, wolves, jackals are always bad. Writers have no mercy. They've been doing tricks like that in books since people began to write. This trick is three thousand years old! In an old story called *Kalila and Dimna*, a jackal did the exact same thing to a lion and a bull who were friends. So if you ask me why I did what I did, I have to tell you that I don't know! A writer made me do it."

"So what happened in your story?" asked Jo again.

"Lots happened. There was a big fight. Now the Prince thinks that the Big Baboon, his dear friend, is dead because of me. So he wants me dead too. It's a shame."

"How can we help?" said Mina.

"You have to think of what happens next. Think of all the stories you know," said Cal.

They all looked at Big Baboon's pale face. He was sicker and didn't mutter again.

Tim and Jo said together: "Think, Mina!"

Jo said, "You make up good stories for me at night. You can think of something."

"Okay," said Mina. "I have read a lot of stories. I think there has to be a magic cure somewhere, which will heal Big Baboon. I don't think it will be easy to get. Do you know of such a cure, Cal?" Cal's eyes began to glimmer in an odd manner.

"Yes!" he said. "There's a magic herb. It grows in a secret place in the western corner of this land. It's so prickly, so full of deadly stingers, that no one has ever

picked it. The person who knows where to go is a hermit who lives in this forest."

"If we can get to the hermit and find the herb, we might help Big Baboon," said Jo.

"It's going to be more tricky than that," said Tim. "Look over there."

Chapter 4: The Firman

HERMIT'S HUT

Mina saw something stir in the bushes. She saw a long, thick tail stirring up the leaves on the ground. Then she saw the eyes.

"Rats!" she said with alarm. "They're everywhere!"

Hundreds of rats were hiding on the forest floor, under the fir and pine needles.

37

Jo took a step back.

The rats had bright, red eyes, and sharp teeth. Some of them were the size of small dogs.

"They want us to run!" said Mina. "I just know it! This is in the story: they want to catch Cal and take him to Prince Panther and demand a reward for finding the bad fox who made all this happen." As she said that, the first rat came out of the shadows of the fir trees and ran at Cal. Then came another and another.

"Don't run away!" shouted Mina. Cal stood still. Rats came at him.

"What do we do?" said Jo.

Mina thought for a long second. "Run at them and run over them," she said. "Go!"

Tim put one firm foot in front of the other. The girls followed. Then Cal followed. They all began to run at the rats. They ran over them. The rats' backs were as hard as rocks. The rats didn't feel the children's feet.

"Eew!" said Jo, and squirmed. "I stood on one!"

The rats stopped running at Cal. They turned and began to move back into the forest.

Suddenly there was a crash. Tim looked up. "Uh oh," he said. "This one's had too much to eat!"

No one had ever seen a rat this size. He was brown and angry and almost as big as a horse. He had spiky whiskers

 and long rat
teeth. His nose
was black and
shiny. From
between two fir
trees, he looked at
the children and
the fox with shiny,
red eyes. Cal

froze. "Oh no," he said softly. "The

Firman!"

Birds in the trees were silent.

"At last I have found you, fox. I and
my Firkins have been looking for you.
Prince Panther will be pleased," said the
giant rat. "I will bring you to him, get a
reward, become his 'friend' and then I
will sneak my way into getting the crown

—for ME and my Firkins! Ha ha ha! This will be the land of the Firkins! Forever!"

This was the first time the children had ever seen a rat smirk. It made them shiver. The Firman's long, sharp teeth looked like knives. Mina and Tim and Jo did not know what to do. Suddenly Cal put his paw over his nose and made a soft sound. The wind began to blow. It blew harder and harder. The fir trees bent. Dust flew everywhere. The girls closed their eyes. When they looked up, someone was standing in front of Tim.

"Who are you?" said Tim.

"I am the hermit of this forest," said an old man with dark eyes.

Mina opened one eye. The hermit looked just like Uncle Toby when he had told them stories so long ago! Jo thought so, too.

"Are you…Uncle Toby, sir?" the girls asked.

"No, no," the hermit said.

"You look just like him," Mina said and rubbed her eyes. "Just a bit older. Did you make all the rats go away?"

Birds began to sing again in the trees.

"Yes," said the hermit. "They don't like the cold wind that I bring. But they will return. Now what can I do for you, Cal the red fox?"

"We need to find the herb that heals everything, the prickly herb that grows in the cold, far western corner of the land," said Cal.

"The first thing you must do is come to my hut," said the hermit. "I can show you the way you need to go, but it will not be easy. Prince Panther is angry. He means to find you, Cal, and punish you."

"Yes," said Cal sadly. "The Firman would eat me right away if he could, and my old friend, Prince Panther, would reward him. He wants me dead, you know. And the Firman wants the crown, as we know."

"We won't let that happen," said Tim. "Come on, let's follow the hermit."

The hermit led the way through the fir trees. At last they came to a small hut.

"In here," he said.

The hut had two firm seats made of wood from the fir trees. The girls sat down. Tim and Cal stood.

"Sorry," said the hermit. "Not too much room in here. I'm always by myself, you see. Now look. Here is a map."

He took a stick and drew a circle in the dirt at their feet. "This is where you are now. Here is the forest all around.

And here is the Glassy Lake, which leads into the Squirmy River.

"When you get to the Glassy Lake, you'll find a small boat. Row over the lake in the boat. Don't stir the water too much, or you'll wake the Water Rats who are just as bad as their brothers, the Firkins. Go down the Squirmy River, but take care. The wild waters will swirl and twirl under your boat and try to tip you over."

"I can't swim very well," said Jo.

"I can," said Cal. "And you can always ride on my back. Now, if we don't get tipped into the river, what will happen?"

"The swirling water will squirt you onto the river bank in the far western corner of this land."

"How will we find the herb then?" said Mina.

"You'll find it," said the hermit. "You must hurry now."

"Yes, let's get there first," said Tim. "Big Baboon is running out of time."

Chapter 5: The Left Turn

Cal and his friends made their way to the Glassy Lake where they found a boat waiting for them on the sandy shore.

"Keep your eyes open for water rats," Tim said and helped Mina and Jo into the boat. Cal hopped in after them. They took turns rowing. The lake was as still as glass.

"Who knows what lurks in this lake," Mina said. "We have to try not to disturb the surface."

A slow current took the boat to the other side of the lake.

"Look!" said Jo. "The Squirmy River!"

The boat took a turn into the first curve of the river. The water was murky. Suddenly a bump and a thump rocked the sturdy boat from side to side.

Now the children could hear the murmur of the river as it went down from the lake, rushing over rocks.

"Look out!" said Tim.

They were rushing towards a set of wild rapids. Water burst over the side of the boat.

"Surf the waves," shouted Tim. He hurled himself to the other side of the boat.

"It's going to turn over!" said Jo. They saw the white crest of a river wave curl over the front of the boat.

The boat gave a lurch from the left to the right. Then it turned upside down and dumped three children and one red fox into the churning water of the Squirmy River.

Down they went into the murky water. Mina was surprised that she didn't feel cold or wet.

When her feet hit the sand at the bottom of the river, she looked up and saw the rapids churning over her head. Then she saw Tim and Cal walking slowly towards her on the river floor.

Jo was behind them.

"Hey!" said Jo, and bubbles came out of her mouth. "What's going on?"

"We're breathing underwater," Mina said, and bubbles came out of her mouth.

"We can't breathe underwater!" Jo said.

"Yes we can," Mina said. "In this story, foxes speak and we breathe underwater and don't get wet!"

"It's hard walking underwater," said Cal. Bubbles came out of his mouth too. "Remember, I have four legs, not two!"

"Let's go with the current," said Tim. "The hermit didn't say what we should do if the boat turned over."

"I say we keep going," said Mina.

"You're making too many bubbles," Jo said. "I can't see where I'm going."

Everyone had to stop talking. They looked at the odd world under the river. Fish swam over them. Weeds grew like grass. There were rocks up ahead on the riverbed, and the river split into two rivers. One river went to the right and the other to the left.

Bubbles came up from the reeds.

"Come and play, children!"

"Who said that?" said Mina.

"A nasty water rat," said Cal.

"Keep going," said Tim. A big, fat, swimming rat shot out from the reeds and went over all their heads.

"Don't be afraid of a silly water rat," said the rat, and bubbles came out of his mouth and stuck to his whiskers. "I'm not going to hurt you. It's fun down here! When was the last time you walked underwater?"

"Never have," said Tim. "Let's keep going."

"Hey, hey," said the rat and swam in front of Tim. "Why so fast? Come and see my home, will you? I haven't had anyone visit me for sooooo long!"

"Wait!" said Jo. "I want to see the water rat's home. Rat, we'd love to see your home. And after our visit, please show us the way to the end of the Squirmy River."

"Oh, yes, yes," said the rat. "Follow me."

"I don't like his red eyes," Mina said softly to Cal, and bubbles came out of her mouth. "They make me feel....dizzy and forgetful..."

The river water was murky and dark. The rat went in front of them and took them down the left turn in the river.

"I can't see very well," Jo said. "Where is your home, rat?"

"Not very far."

At last they came to the rat's home. He had a lovely spot in the reeds. His house was very grand. It was all made of river rocks. In the murky water, one by one, the children forgot why they were going down the Squirmy River. The rat looked at them with his bright red eyes and said, "Please stay. Why do you want to get to the end of the river? Why not just stay here, with me?"

Cal's fur stood on end under the water. "It's a trap," he said to Mina. "Let's go."

"Go where?" said Mina.

"To get the herb to heal Big Baboon!"

"Who's that?" said Mina.

"Oh no!" said Cal. "The water rats work for the Firman. They've made you forget everything. They know that if we heal Big Baboon, the prince will be so full of joy that the Firman will never get close to the prince. The Firman will only get to the prince if Big Baboon is dead and he can bring me, the bad fox, to Prince Panther."

"Who's the Firman?" said Jo. "Hey, rat, got anything to eat? I'm hungry!"

Cal got angry. He ran to Jo and bit her leg. "You forgot!" he snapped.

"Ouch!"

He ran to Tim and bit his leg.

"Ow!"

He was about to bite Mina.

"Wait!" said Tim. "I remember! This isn't the way the story should go. We've got to get out of here!" He grabbed Mina and Jo and pulled them away from the water rat's home.

Chapter 6: By the Light of the Moon

It was hard to run fast in the water, but the water rat did not follow them. He could not make them stay if they didn't want to.

"We've been fools," Mina said. "We could have been stuck there forever. We forgot what we were doing. Wait! Is this water getting cool?"

"Yes. I'm cold," said Jo.

"I think it gets colder as we go west," said Mina.

"What's that?" said Tim pointing up.

They all looked up at the top of the river. Afternoon had faded to night. The moon was big and round over the water.

"It's ice," Cal said.

"Ice on the river," said Tim. "We really have to get out of here fast!"

As the water grew dark and cold, the children could see ice chunks drift by. It was hard to walk and their mood was gloomy.

"If we can make it to the river bank, we can just get out," said Tim.

"I'm too cold," said Jo. "I can't go on."

Tim took Jo's hand and Cal went ahead. The current was strong. "We're almost there!" said Tim.

"There's no room to get out," Mina said. "It's all ice. I'm getting stuck!"

Then she saw an old rope lying on the riverbed. She took hold of it and gave a tug. It was stuck firmly in the riverbank.

Tim made a loop with the rope. He began to pull himself toward the riverbank. The others came after him. Cal held the rope with his teeth.

Tim was first to get out of the river. He stood on the bank in the cool wind under the light of the moon.

Cal and Jo and Mina got out next. They were cold and wet. The river had frozen over.

"That was a bit too spooky for me," said Tim.

"Me too," said Jo. "Now what?"

"Hey, look, our boat!" Mina said. "It's stuck in the ice! We can't do anything with it anyway."

Tim still held the loop of the rope in his hand. "I think this could work," he said. He went onto the ice and had to stoop over the boat.

"Watch out!" said Mina. "The ice is thin."

Tim looped the rope around the boat and gave a tug. The boat slid out of the ice toward the children.

"Get in," said Tim.

Cal said, "We can shoot down the Squirmy River on the ice and get there sooner."

"Get WHERE sooner?" said Jo.

"Out of this gloomy place," said Cal, and he got into the boat.

Tim, Jo and Mina got in after Cal. The boat began to slide on the ice. The river was smooth and white in the light of the full moon.

"Did we choose the right turn in the river, and is there still time to save Big Baboon?" Mina asked Cal.

"I hope so," said Cal.

The boat slid along the ice for some time.

The Squirmy River ended in a big, frozen pool. The boat slid onto the smooth pool. The children got out. They had to walk on the ice and scoot the boat to the edge of the pool. They left it there and stepped onto cold, snowy ground.

Jo sat down in a bad mood. "I'm cold, and I need some food."

"Well," said Tim. "Lucky for you, the hermit gave me this." He took out a brown bag from under his shirt.

"What's that?" Jo asked.

"Don't drool too much! It's bread and cheese and nuts and apples."

"Food!" said Mina.

"Yum!" said Jo.

Jo took some bread and cheese and sat down on the snowy ground. "Ouch!" she said and jumped up. A bright yellow flower bloomed in the snow. It was the most prickly plant that any of them had ever seen.

"It's the herb!" Cal shouted as he sniffed the plant. "The herb that heals and gives life! We've got it!"

But the plant was so prickly that no one could get at it. Mina dug around it, but she could not get it. Jo's hands got sore from trying to grab it.

"We can't do it," said Tim.

Then Cal began to dig around it until he got under the long, thin taproot. He dug that up.

"You've got it!" said Tim. He pulled the plant out by its root and put it in the brown bag. Holding it open he said, "We can keep it in this."

Cal came over, took the herb by the root, in his mouth, and put it in the bag. Then Tim put the bag back under his shirt.

"We did it, Cal!" he said. "We got the herb!"

Mina ate her bread and cheese, and Jo ate too.

Suddenly, there was a loud BOOM! The ground shook.

They looked up and saw a big shadow cross the moon.

"The Firman!" Mina said.

"So you've come to my lagoon!" boomed the Firman. "Ha ha!" The jumbo-sized rat with the nasty grin loomed over them.

"Buffoons!" he cried. "Nincompoops! Did you really think you could get away?"

He reached down and grabbed Cal. "Whoopee!" he said, lifting the little fox in his big claws. "Got you now. We're off to my igloo. For dinner. Yum Yum!"

As he walked into the dark woods, Mina stood up and cried: "You're the Buffoon! You're the Nincompoop!"

Chapter 7: From Woods to Moor

"Poor Cal," Jo said, and began to cry.

"We'll get him back," Mina said.

"Let's start to look for him right now," said Tim and stood up tall. "The Firman went that way, into the dark woods. Let's go!"

They took off after the Firman in the moonlight. A thin dusting of snow lay on the ground so they could see the Firman's footprints.

They went through the woods, and out onto an icy moor.

A big igloo stood in the moor.

"It's his igloo!" said Tim. "And look, I think Cal's in there." He pointed to an old woodshed next to the igloo. Jo looked through the holes in the sides of the woodshed.

"That's Cal!" she cried. "How do we get him out of there?"

"What a good-for-nothing Crookneck Boor that Firman is!" a voice said.

"Who said that?" said Mina.

"I did," said a small, furry beaver. "I saw your tracks in the snow next to the river, and I came after you. Did you know that Firman and his bunch of Firkins are up to no good?" he said. "They want to take over this land." The beaver looked at the woodshed.

"It's lucky for you and your fox friend, that I'm good with wood."

Mina said, "Can you get Cal out?"

"Got to give it a try," said the beaver, "or the Firman will cook your poor friend and eat him!"

"Cook him?" said Jo. "No!"

"The Firman wants to be king of the world," said the beaver. "Every other animal is afraid of him. But, I'm not."

"If the Firman were to cook poor Cal, this would not make a good story or a good book," Mina said.

"By hook or by crook, I will get him out," said the beaver. "As I said, I'm good with wood! Look at me go!"

The beaver took his time creeping over the moor. His wide tail left a trail in the snow. He went to the woodshed and hid in a nook by the side.

Jo shook. "Look," she said.

Hooking his teeth into the wood, the beaver began to do what beavers do best—chew wood!

Soon the beaver took some wood off the side of the shed.

There was a gap in the woodshed, and Cal dashed out.

He and the beaver ran fast through the snow and over the moor.

"Cal!" Jo cried with joy as the red fox trotted up to the children.

"Oh no! Look!" Cried Tim. "The Firman's out of his igloo! Run to the woods!"

They made it deep into the woods, but the Firman followed. His footsteps shook the ground where they stood.

"Where can we hide?" said Mina.

"My place," said the beaver. "Run."

The woods were very dark and they could not see well at all. Finally they got out of the woods, but they could still feel footsteps that shook them.

"Cooky, hookneck crookman!" said the beaver. "You will not get us!"

Next to the banks of the frozen Squirmy River, the beaver made a dash for a nook in the reeds. "In here," he said.

Tim, Mina, Cal, and Jo went after him.

"Look at this," said Cal. "Thank you, beaver. Are we safe now?"

They were in the beaver's small, dark, damp home.

"For a bit," he said. "The Firman will not be able to look in here. He's too big. Eats too much, I say! But the sun will be up soon, and you must get away from here. Where are you going?"

"To the hermit's house. To the woods where Big Baboon is," said Mina. "Can we go back up the Squirmy River?"

Big loud footsteps went past the beaver's home.

"I don't think so," said the beaver softly. "Follow me west through the woods. I can show you where to go. But we must hurry or the sun will be up."

Suddenly Mina said to Tim: "What about the herb?"

Jo and Cal and the beaver looked at Tim.

Tim took a brown bag out of his shirt. "I've got it in here," he said. There it was: the prickly herb that could heal all.

They waited a long time. At last the footsteps of the Firman faded away.

"He must be very mad that he lost his dinner," said Jo.

"Which was a good thing for me," said Cal.

It was getting light as they made their way through the woods. They had to go west for a long time. At last the sun began to come up, and they stopped at a river.

"It's the Squirmy River!" said Mina.

"There's no more ice," said Tim.

"It only gets cold far to the west where the Firman lives," said the beaver. "You can follow the river now. It will take you to the Glassy Lake."

"Thank you, Beaver. I will never forget you," said Cal.

The beaver gave a wave with his tail and jumped into the river. The children and Cal went on through the woods.

"Have we seen this before?" said Jo.

"Yes. It's the Glassy Lake," said Mina. The water was as still as glass. "Pity we lost the boat," she said.

They went on through the woods. Suddenly they saw something in the sunlight under a big fir tree. It was very still.

"Big Baboon!" They all said.

Chapter 8: A Foul Trick

"He looks dead," said Jo sadly.

Cal sat down next to Big Baboon.
Tim let the herb drop out of the bag
onto the ground.

The herb had a small, yellow flower.
Cal gave the herb a push with his nose
until it was under Big Baboon's nose. The
children had to crouch around Big

Baboon. First there was no sound. Then Big Baboon gave a loud sniff!

"Wow!" said Jo, "He's alive! Not a scrape or even a cut on him! We did it Cal!"

Big Baboon got up. He was very drowsy, so he fell down again and landed on the prickly herb. "Ouch!" he shouted. His eye fell on Cal.

"What's this?" he growled. Cal looked down.

"It's the herb we found to heal you."

Big Baboon began to glower. He looked at Mina and Tim and Jo. Then he glared at Cal.

"You made the Prince my enemy," said Big Baboon.

"Cal's very sorry," said Tim. "He came all the way to our land to get help."

"Oh, did he?" said Big Baboon loudly with a scowl. "Now how do I make this fox clown pay for what he did?"

"Please don't shout," said Mina. "You must be feeling a bit sour, but allow Cal to speak."

"Go on," said Big Baboon. "The panther, the Crown Prince, is my enemy forever, thanks to Cal."

"Not so," said Cal. "After the big fight, Prince Panther found me out. He wept for days. He thought you were dead. Then

81

he wanted me dead. I thought it was the end for us all. And then I found a way out of this land. I had to howl for many nights, for a long time, to rouse Mina from her sleep."

"And me!" said Jo. "You had to rouse me too, Cal."

"We heard his howls so we came down through a secret door into your land," said Mina.

"Cal is your friend," said Tim. "He saved your life."

Big Baboon's mouth fell open. "Prince Panther wept for me?" he said.

"Yes," said Cal. "I made an error, don't ask me why. Prince Panther would give his crown to see you alive again!"

"Oh my," said Big Baboon. His round, brown eyes began to fill with tears.

He was still drowsy, but he sat down on the ground and began to pound his chest. "Power to the Prince," he shouted. "Take me there, Cal. Now!"

Cal gave a flick of his tail and stood up. Mina and Tim helped Big Baboon to his feet. He began to stomp around with joy.

"Let's go!" shouted Mina.

By now they were a loud and rowdy bunch making their way through the woods. They didn't hear the sound of many other little feet behind them.

"Rats!!!" shouted Tim. From every part of the woods came the Firkins, big rats and small rats. Cal ran up to one rat and bit him. Tim wasn't afraid. He ran to the rats to beat them back. But Cal and Tim were no match for the Firkins.

"Got this one now!" a Firkin yelled. Five of them held Cal down.

"What a crowd we have here! Got the boy, too!" Seven other Firkins wound Tim and Cal tightly with rope. Mina was too scared to make a sound. The rats pulled Tim and Cal fast over the ground. Then, a big crash resounded through the woods.

"Good work, boys," scowled the Firman. "Now we have two! Ha ha ha."

With that, Cal and Tim and all the rats and the Firman were gone.

"How could this happen?" said Jo, and burst into tears.

"Now, now, all is not lost," a voice said.

Mina and Jo and Big Baboon looked up to see the hermit. His deep brown eyes were kind.

Jo wiped her wet cheeks. "Uncle Toby, is that you?" she said.

"No, just the hermit," said the hermit with a smile. "I saw that foul trick. I cannot fight the Firman, but I do have friends around in these woods. Let us see what we can do. No need to give up. Not yet."

"Thanks uncle To…I mean, thank you, sir," said Mina.

The hermit took Mina and Jo's hands in his. "Take Big Baboon over the plain to the rocky cave in the mountain where Prince Panther lives."

"I know the way," said Big Baboon.

"Good," said the hermit. "Tell the prince the story."

"Yes," said Big Baboon. "He will have the story. Come my friends, follow me."

The hermit went into the woods. The girls followed Big Baboon out of the woods and onto the big, wide plain. The sun was high in the sky. It felt very hot after the cool shade of the trees.

"Can you see where we are?" said Mina to Jo.

"I think so," said Jo. "When we left the cellar, the moon was up, so it didn't look like this. Is that the hill that goes to our...our...?"

"Cellar? I think so," said Mina.

"What's a cellar?" said Big Baboon. He kept looking around for rats.

"It's just a place," said Mina. "We live close to it."

"Good," said Big Baboon. "Do you see that mountain in the south?"

"Yes!" said the girls.

"The prince lives there."

"How do we get up to the cave?" said Jo.

"With my help," said Big Baboon.

Chapter 9: The Boy and the Fox

At the other end of the plain, a big rocky cliff cast a shadow on the ground. Mina and Jo looked up and saw the dark mouth of a cave.

In the shade of the cliff, the soil under their feet was moist and cool. "What about Tim and Cal?" said Jo and her voice shook.

"Makes my blood boil," said Big

Baboon. "I just got round to feeling thankful, and then that oily rat came to spoil things."

"The hermit will help. He said so. And we have to get to Prince Panther to tell him."

"Big Baboon, how in the world are we to get up that cliff?" said Jo. "Our friends' lives depend on it."

"The back way, and the side way," he said. "We go out of the shadows, into the sun. It's the secret way into the royal abode."

Big Baboon began to enjoy himself. He went around the steep side of the cliff and the girls followed.

"This is steep for a person, but nothing for Big Baboon. Hold onto my tail, both of you. Ouch! Not so hard. There, now I can hoist you up!"

The soil was rocky and sandy, but Big Baboon was strong. His tail was a very good rope. Soon they came to a big, flat rock.

"Ouch, ouch, you can let go of my poor tail now," he said.

The rock was hot from the sun, and Mina's feet began to burn through her shoes.

"Sorry," she said. "Where's the cave?"

"Right under us," said Big Baboon. "Just over there is a hole in the rock. It's not very wide, but a small girl or a Big Baboon could fit into it.

The hole leads into the royal cave—the back way."

They ran to the hole and peeked in. It was as dark as night in there. They could smell damp soil.

"Girls first," said Big Baboon. "And you have a choice. You can jump or slide. It's some ride into that deep, dark void!"

"I'll go," said Mina and sat on the edge of the hole with her legs hanging down into it.

"Now, please, you must be as good as any loyal subject. Do not annoy Prince Panther. Be polite when you get there."

"I will," said Mina and slid in. "Yikes! It is a deep, dark void!"

"Not so much noise. Shhh," said Big Baboon.

Mina slid fast down a tunnel with Jo right behind. They landed with two bumps at the back of a big, wide, cave. On a rock overlooking the plain, lay the black Prince Panther. He turned his royal head so that the girls saw his golden crown.

"What do we have here?" he said. "Children? From the world beyond? How is this?"

Big Baboon came crashing down the tunnel into Mina's back. "May I join you?" he said.

Prince Panther got up on all fours and looked at the three of them with deep, yellow eyes. His voice shook when he spoke.

"Big Baboon, is that you? Are you not dead?"

"As far as I can see, I'm alive," said Big Baboon. The prince gave a howl of joy.

"Did I not destroy you?" said Prince Panther. "Did Cal, that pointy-tailed fox not destroy us with his tricks? I will have him boiled…"

"No!" said Mina. "There's more to the story! He saved Big Baboon. He came to get us."

"Really? I must ask Big Baboon; but first, I must check that this IS Big Baboon."

The prince jumped off the rock and came to inspect Big Baboon. "It is you," he said. "My dear friend, my most loyal friend. Where's the fox?"

"The Firman has him. And he has our friend Tim, too!" said Mina in a tiny voice.

"What does the Firman want?" asked the prince. He was so big and dark and wild that Mina and Jo began to shake.

"He wants to bring you the fox who made you fight with Big Baboon," Jo said. "And he has Tim because Tim tried to stop him from taking us all."

At that moment there was a noise far down on the plain. Prince Panther shook off his royal crown and bounded to the end of the cave. His voice boomed across the land as Mina, Jo, and Big Baboon ran to the end of the cave to see.

"Ah. The boy and the fox!" said the prince.

"Good day, your Royal...um, Catness," said the Firman. He stood on the plain with a sea of rats around his feet. Cal and Tim sat, looking very sad indeed, in a big, wooden crate. "I hope you will appoint me the Best Royal Help Ever," said the Firman. "For I have here, none other than Cal the red fox and his friend. This is the fox who made such a mess of your life, your Royal, um, Cat..."

"I'm a panther, thank you, Firman," said the prince.

"I did this for you," said the big rat. "I've come for my royal spoils," said the Firman. "Right boys?" he said to his rats. There was a rushing noise as all the rats agreed. They ran all over the crate and some got on top of it.

"What?" said the prince, and his royal eyes became gold slits in the sun. "Did I tell you to get Cal?"

"Nooo," said the Firman, slowly. "But we did it for you, Prince Panther."

"You're beginning to annoy me," said the prince. "You did it for you. For what you could get out of it. Now, Big Baboon, the girl said there was more to the story."

"Yes, yes," said Big Baboon. "In fact, Cal the fox did save me—he and these children. They found the herb that heals all, and it gave me new life."

"So," said Prince Panther. "I have my dear friend with me again, thanks to Cal. In that case, Firman, open the crate, and let the fox and the boy go."

"No, no, no!" said the Firman. "I know what he did, and I'm not letting him go! I need a reward."

Chapter 10: The Reward

There was a pause. Prince Panther stood and put up his front paw. "Firman, I tell you, do not cause me to get angry. Let the fox and the boy go!"

Mina and Jo and Big Baboon watched the Firman turn to his rats, the Firkins. "He wants us to give him the fox and the boy, with no reward. What do you say, boys?"

"Be an outlaw," said one. "Let's take them back into the woods. Let's demand our reward!"

"Reward or no fox," came the taunt from the rat crowd. "Reward, or no boy!"

The children and Big Baboon saw the panther drop his jaw and give a big yawn. He held up his paw again. This time, Mina saw his awful, sharp claws. These were claws that could maul anything, but the Firman went on singing his taunts:

> It was Cal the fox's fault,
> We saw the fight, the jaws and
> claws
> Now we'll lock him in a vault
> Till we get our just reward!

Mina saw Tim's face. It was pale and drawn. Jo held her hand.

"It's awful," she said.

Suddenly, at the far end of the plain, the hermit appeared.

"Withdraw to your frozen corner of the land," said Prince Panther to the Firkins. The hermit clapped his hands. The children watched in awe. Big cats of every kind began to come down onto the plain. Lions with their tawny hides and big claws came down from the cliffs, as did cheetahs and panthers. The rats saw the big cats, and they began to run backwards. They forgot about the fox and Tim as the big cats launched themselves at the Firman and his Firkins.

"At last, a cat big enough to go after the Firman," said Mina to Jo, as the tawny lion vaulted after him into the woods.

Cal and Tim sat in the crate in the hot sun and looked up at the cave.

"Let them out," said the prince. The hermit broke open the crate and let Tim and Cal out onto the plain.

Then all the cats came back from the woods. There was a big round of applause as Cal and Tim and the hermit began to make their way towards the cave.

Mina turned to Prince Panther. "Where are the rats, your majesty?" she asked in a small voice.

103

"My dear girl, they are banished to the far western corner of the land. They will stay there, bound in by ice and snow all year round."

"Can they get out?"

"Not as long as I am prince," said Prince Panther. "My cats will take care of that."

Mina said, "Just so you know, it wasn't Cal's fault."

"What do you mean?" said Prince Panther.

"He didn't want to cause all this. An author made him do it."

"An author? Is that an animal?" said the prince.

"No. An author is a person who writes books."

"Why would a person do such a thing?"

"I don't know, and that's the truth," said Mina. "But Cal is a good fox, and he got us here to help."

At the back of the cave, Cal and Tim and the hermit came in. Jo and Mina ran to pet Cal and hug Tim.

"Big Baboon and hermit, are these your friends?" said the prince.

"Yes, Sir," said Big Baboon. "They saved my life."

"In that case, they are my friends too," said the prince. "We must find this author person who caused all this."

"I'll find him," said Mina.

"Good," said Prince Panther. "What do you have to say for yourself, Cal the fox?"

"Thank you, sir. I am so glad that I was not mauled and eaten by those outlaws. It was awful in that crate. All I wanted was to save Big Baboon and bring him back to you safe and sound."

"It's done," said the hermit. "My work is done too. I must be off to the woods. Good-bye all."

"Thank you hermit," said Tim. "I knew you'd get us back here safely. We should go too."

The children suddenly saw that all the big cats were lying in a shadow at the back of the cave. The tawny lion gave a yawn and then stood up. "I'll take you back," he said to the hermit. "And my friend here can escort the children home." He nodded at the cheetah by his side. The hermit climbed onto the lion's back, and held on. Then the lion jumped out of the cave and ran down the steep rocky cliff. The children waved at the hermit, but he was holding on so tightly he could not wave back.

"My friends," said Prince Panther as he sat between Cal and Big Baboon. "These two are true friends. And you three I count as friends too. I will never

again listen to words against friends—
words that do not feel true in my heart."

The sun had almost set. The
children stood up.

"We need to get back before
dawn," said Mina. She did not know how
long they had been away. It felt like a
very, very long time.

"Find the author," said Prince
Panther.

Mina nodded. "I will," she said.

Chapter 11: By the Glow of the Moon

"Show them the way," Prince Panther said to the sleek spotted cheetah.

"Yes, sir," said the cheetah. She got up and they saw how big she was. "You can ride on my back," she said. Then she bent down low. Jo got on first, then Mina, and then Tim.

"Will we ever see you again, Cal?" said Mina, who wanted to cry.

"I don't know," said Cal. "I think this is happily ever after."

"Hold on!" said the cheetah to the children, and like an arrow from a bow, she shot out of the cave.

"Bye," shouted Cal and Big Baboon.

They landed on a narrow path, which they had to follow. The cliff was so steep that the children thought they would never make it down. The path was overgrown and lit up by the moon. When they looked back, they saw the shadows of Prince Panther, Big Baboon and Cal at the mouth of the cave.

"The moon's full again," said Jo. "Have we been gone for a month?"

"It can't be!" said Mina.

"Well, how long have we been here?" said Jo.

"A few days maybe?" said Tim.

"Can't be!" said Mina.

In the glow of the moon, the children saw a shadow creeping low on the ground and they held tightly to the cheetah's fur.

"Stop!" said a voice.

They came to a willow by a shallow stream. The shadow followed them. "Stop. S.T.O.P!"

"Who is it?" said Tim.

"Show a bit of respect for this old fellow," said the shadow. "Don't go home without saying goodbye."

"Beaver!" shouted Jo.

"You're all a bit slow," said the beaver. Mina smiled.

"Did you forget the snow?" he said.

"Never!" said Jo.

"I wish you could borrow me," said the beaver. "I wish I could follow you home, come in your window, and sleep on your pillow. But I have to stay in my own land."

"And I wish I could borrow you," said Jo. "But we each belong in our own lands."

"See you, Beaver!" said Jo. "Thank you for the kindness you've shown!"

The beaver waved his flat tail. His low shadow went slowly towards the shallow stream. Then in he went, following the flow of the water to his home in the reeds.

When they came to the rocky hill and saw that the moon was as round as a glowing bowl, Tim said, "Thank you, Cheetah. We get off here." The children jumped off her back.

"Good work," said the cheetah. All is well in this land."

Mina put her hand on the cheetah's soft head. "That was a good ride," she said.

"Ouch! I just cut my leg on a rock," said Jo.

The cheetah brushed against Jo's cut. The cut stopped hurting. Then she looked at the children. "May the winds blow you back here some day," she said. Her eyes seemed to glow in the moon-light. Then she dashed into the shadows, and they stood there on their own— Mina, Jo and Tim.

"What now?" Jo said.

"We go up the hill," said Mina.

"Over the rocks, by the light of the moon," said Tim. "The same way we came here."

They made their way over the rocks and up the hill. The wind blew cool. They could smell dampness. When they looked over the plain they could see the low grass, the far woods, the willow and the shallow stream. The cliff with Prince Panther's deep cave hollow cast a stark shadow on the ground even from so far away.

"What if we can't get home?" said Jo. "I don't see steps, I don't see the cellar, I don't..."

"Slow down," said Tim. "Look at your feet."

Jo and Mina looked at their feet. Under their feet they saw steps. Looking back, they saw a wall, and on the side, a trunk filled with old books. In front of them, over them, the children saw the cellar door. There was a glow of moonlight through the cracks in the wood. They had come back through the secret door.

Mina pushed the trapdoor to the workshop open. Moonlight from the window lit her face as she climbed up into the old workshop. Soon Jo came out of the cellar with Tim. They stood there, in their own land, under pale moonlight.

"What day is it?" Tim said.

"What time is it?" Mina said.

"We'd better get to bed," Jo said. They walked out into the yard where the grass was wet and cool. "Well, the grass hasn't grown," said Tim. "We haven't been gone for a month."

A window opened. "Mina? Jo? What are you doing out there so late?"

"Nothing, Dad," Jo said. "We thought Tim's dog was in the cellar."

"In the cellar? Goodness me. Well, was he?"

"Nope," said Mina. "No dogs there. Tim's at home now. What time is it, Dad?"

"It's nine thirty. You'd best get back to bed, children."

"Okay, Dad," Mina and Jo said.

"Nine-thirty?" said Tim with big eyes. "We left at five past nine. We've been away for exactly twenty-five minutes!"

"Yikes," said Jo.

"See you tomorrow, Tim. Sleep well," said Mina. "We'd better go."

Chapter 12: Treachery and Treasure

The sun was already up when Mina awoke. Jo's head was far under her bedspread. The weather was warm. It was a pleasant day.

"Wake up, sleepyhead," said Mina. "Was last night real, or was it a dream? I have to tell you something. It's about Uncle Toby's books."

Jo gave a low growl from under the bedspread. "Let me sleep," she said.

"It can't be real, Jo, can it? I think I had a dream about you and me and Tim and Cal the fox, who did something treacherous, and a dreadful big rat called the Firman…"

Jo poked her head out from the bedspread. "Yes, and it was about Big Baboon, who was almost dead… it was about Prince Panther finding out that the real threat was not Cal the fox, but the Firman and the Firkins. It was real."

"Wow," said Mina. "How do we know that?"

"We were in the realm of Uncle Toby's stories. Look, I still have a scratch on my leg."

Mina looked at Jo's leg.

"Hey, remember! At first you were the one who thought I'd made Cal the fox up," said Mina.

"Well, you didn't," said Jo. "Now I know. And now that story ends…"

"Happily ever after," said Mina. "I have to get a letter to Uncle Toby."

"But he doesn't write," said Jo.

"Well, he can read what I write, can't he?" said Mina.

At breakfast, Mina said, "Mom, where does Uncle Toby live?"

"Far away, across the Pacific Ocean, Mina. He lives in Australia in a hut near a big meadow. He's like a hermit. A long time ago he wrote all the time. But then he lost heart and gave up. For many years he has not written a word. You can send him a letter, but he won't write back. He never writes back to your dad or to me. I have to call the lady who lives next door to him if I want to find out how he is."

"Why is he like that?" Jo said.

"A long time ago," their mom said, "all he dreamed of doing was writing. But his words fell on deaf ears. No one wanted his books."

"Our ears weren't deaf," said Mina. "We loved his stories!" As their mother smiled, Mina and Jo got up. They helped to clear the breakfast table. Then they ran outside to find Tim.

Tim rubbed his eyes and scratched his head.

"I'm so tired," he said. "I had crazy dreams last night."

"They were real," said Mina. "Look at Jo's leg. She scratched herself as she got off the cheetah's back."

"It's true…" said Tim slowly. His eyes grew big, and wide awake.
"Yes. It's all true. The cheetah, Big Baboon, the Squirmy River," said Mina.

"We were there," said Tim. "So that's why I'm so tired."

"And we helped Cal find the herb that heals all," said Jo. "And win his friends back. Do you think the Firman will really spend his life paying for his treachery?"

"It has to be that way," said Mina, "So the story ends happily ever after. The Firman never comes back, and Cal and Big Baboon and Prince Panther are friends forever. We'll never go back there. The story is done."

"Let's get your Uncle Toby's notebook," said Tim.

"What?" Jo looked at him.

"You have to write the ending of the story, Mina," he said. "Uncle Toby's old book has all these empty pages. Write what happens, and write the ending. Then the story of Cal the Red Fox can be read by anyone."

"Okay," said Mina, and she was silent for a moment. Then they ran across the yard to the workshop. Mina opened the trap door.

She went down the steps into the old musty cellar with the trunk of notebooks. She took the story of Cal the

125

Red Fox out of the trunk. She looked at the cellar walls and saw nothing beyond them. They were old and damp. There was no Secret Door into another land. The story of Cal the Red Fox was now in Mina's hands.

Back in the house, Mina wrote the story as it had happened. She read it to Tim and Jo. "Tell me if I've written it right," she said. "I don't want to leave anything out."

When she came to the end, Jo spoke up: "You forgot to write about the scratch on my leg."

"Okay," said Mina. "I'll add that." When she had finished, she closed the book and took it to her room where she had a treasure box. With care, she slowly put the story of Cal the Red Fox into the box and shut the lid. She sat for a moment, thinking. Then she took out some writing paper.

Jo popped her head in the room. "Let's go and play outside," she said.

"Not now," Mina said.

"Why, what are you going to write now?" Jo asked.

"I told Prince Panther that I would write to the author of the story. So I will."

"Are you going to ask him why he made Cal the fox do such a dreadful thing?" Jo asked.

"I could, but he may never write back," Mina said. "Let me think for a bit."

Tim and Jo ran outside to play and Mina spread out all her pens. Then she began to write with her best pen, in purple ink on white paper.

September 5,

Dear Uncle Toby,
I know you don't write anymore, so if you never write back to me, that's okay. I won't expect a reply. I want to tell you, though, that I know what happens at the end of the story about Cal the Red Fox.

You never finished that story, and poor Cal was left in a dreadful state. If I ever see you again I will tell you everything. I can tell you a bit now:

Tim and Jo and I found a secret door in the cellar. Beyond the secret door lay the realm of Cal and Big Baboon and the Firman and the Firkins and Beaver and hermit and the big cats. We went into that world hardly trusting that it was true. At the end, Prince Panther wanted to know what we all wanted to know, so I have to ask: why did you make Cal, the sweet fox, do treacherous things to his friends? Why did the fox have to be bad? Well, luckily I can tell you that Cal the red fox and Big Baboon and Prince Panther become friends again. I know. I was there with

Tim and Jo, and we saw the real end happen in front of our eyes. I wrote it all down, so your book is finished at last, and Cal and Big Baboon and Prince Panther all do live happily ever after.

Love, your niece

Mina

THE END